This book is a collection of recipes I made suitable for my little man with cow's protein intolerance.

This is little man Jacob when he was 7 months old, he was doing very well as we found him a vegan formula that didn't set off his allergies.

It was Hipp Organic before the recipe change; it was a couple of weeks after this with the new recipe that he got sick with his allergy.

He's a cute little chunk, I know, he's twelve on his next birthday, which is crazy and unfortunately, he hasn't grown out of his cow's milk protein intolerance. He hasn't outgrown the allergy because he just doesn't have the digestive enzyme that breaks down milk sugars.

They are all great bakes, treats and meals. We soon began thinking about a whole diet change for his health that wouldn't be terrible for the whole family including my vegetarian husband, so I came up with delicious meals that won't make you or your little one ill.

I was inspired to write this book one night about a year after Jacob's diagnosis, hubby and I were watching television and something came on about fresh start and the importance of calcium which made me smile as only that morning I has taken my son to be weighed and to our joy he was back on his birth curve despite not eating any dairy for a whole year.

I had given some details of recipes I had made for Jacob to the health visitor and they'd been surprised by my ingenuity; this got me thinking that there would be other parents struggling the way I first did with meal times feeling like a mine field. This made me decide that sharing my recipes could be beneficial to others not just to Jacob.

All the next recipes feed a family of four unless otherwise stated.

## Flapjacks

*Makes 30*

150g/ 6 oz dairy free margarine
100g/ 4 oz/ 6 tbsp clear honey
200g/ 8 oz caster sugar
350g/ 12 oz rolled oats

Melt the dairy free margarine with the honey and the caster sugar; then stir in the rolled oats.

Press the mixture into a greased 30cm/ 12 in by 20cm/ 8 in tin.

Bake in a pre-heated oven at 180°C/ 350°F/ gas mark 4 for about 20 minutes until lightly golden.

Leave to cool slightly before cutting, and then leave in the tin until cool on a cooling rack before turning out.

*One of Jacob's favourites, he can now make them too because he watched me making them so often that he has learned the recipe.*

## Fig Bars

*Makes 16*

225g/ 8 oz fresh figs, chopped
30 ml/ 2 tbsp clear honey
15 ml/ 1 tbsp lemon juice
225g/ 8 oz wholemeal flour
225g/ 8 oz rolled oats
225g/ 8 oz dairy free margarine
75g/ 3 oz soft brown sugar

Simmer the figs, honey and lemon juice over a low heat for 5 minutes, then allow to cools slightly.

Mix together the flour and the oats, then rub in the dairy free margarine and stir in the sugar.

Press half of the mixture into a greased 20 cm/ 8 in square cake tin, then spoon in the fig mixture over the top.

Cover with the remaining mixture and press down firmly.

Bake in a pre-heated oven at 180°C/ 350°F/ gas mark 4 for about 30 minutes until golden brown.

Leave to cool slightly before cutting into bars, leave in the tin to cool slightly, cut into slices while still warm.

**Grandma Ruth's Victoria Sandwich Cake,
Made into cupcakes.**

Makes 24 cupcakes or fairy cakes

175g/ 6 oz dairy free margarine
175g/ 6 oz super fine caster sugar
3 eggs, beaten
175g/ 6 oz of self-raising flour

Beat the dairy free margarine until soft

Cream in the sugar until pale and fluffy

Gradually beat in the eggs

Fold in the flour

Divide the mixture evenly, I use dessert spoons into 24 cupcake cases
Bake in a preheated oven at 190°C/ 375°F/ gas mark 5 for about 20 minutes until well
risen and springy to the touch.

Allow to cool on a wire rack, only when completely cool can you decorate with dairy
free icing

**Dairy free Butter Icing**

Makes enough to cover 24 cupcakes/ also enough to fill and cover 1 20cm/ 8 in cake

125g/ 4 oz dairy free margarine
250g/ 8 oz icing sugar sifted
Less milk if you use vanilla extract
5 - 7ml/ 1-1 1/2 tbsp soya milk

Beat the dairy free margarine until soft

Gradually beat in the icing sugar and the soya milk until well blended

Smooth over the cake or pipe on to the cupcakes.

*I made many trays of cupcakes to get the exactly right, and the way I wanted them. Soft and springy and sweet, it was a lot of trial and error, but we love this recipe and have obviously made these many times.*

*The cupcakes with the blue sparkles were made for Jacob's birthday, they were vanilla flavour with dairy free butter cream icing.*

*The green and pink iced cupcakes were for a birthday tea party I planned for Jacob and his Grandma Anne in the middle of their birthdays as there is only 2 weeks between.*

*Mum's were decorated in pink and silver with delicate rose buds on the top of the icing and Jacob's are mint green with little orange rugby balls made from icing.*

*The last set of cupcakes are from Easter that year, we couldn't find a huge supple of dairy free chocolate eggs, so I bought a small bag and used them to decorate lemon flavoured cupcakes with the same recipe. Jacob also helped to stamp the flowers out of fondant icing.*

*The pretty orange flavour cupcakes to the left were for a hamper prize I made for a school fare at Jacob's primary school.*

*I added orange juice to the cake batter and orange extract to the icing as well as the rind used to decorate the rosettes on the top of the cake.*

*There was also banana in the icing sugar, these cupcakes were moreish and followed the cake recipe for a Victoria sponge from my Grandma.*

*The cake in this photo was a Victoria sponge I made using the recipe, the mixture sometimes needs a small amount of dairy free single cream, which depends on the warmth of the dairy free margarine being used. I made this cake for my Mum's birthday.*

*The cupcakes to the left I made for Mother's Day these were the same recipe from my grandmother with the orange flavouring in the cake and vanilla frosting.*

*My beautiful Grandmother or Grandma Ruth. We were so close as a family, after my parents separated, we lived with our Grandma and Grandad.*

*Grandma Ruth and Grandad Frank are pictured below together.*

*Both of my grandparents were amazing in the kitchen, I loved Grandma Ruth's cooking and baking.*

*My Grandad cooked too, we used to love when Mum and Grandma were out, and Grandad made our dinner. He used to make the best fritta's, sliced fried potato. He called it a Francis's Special.*

# Mummy's Dairy free Chocolate cupcakes

Makes 36 cupcakes

170g/ 6 oz dairy free margarine
170g/ 6 0z caster sugar
3 eggs beaten
10 ml/ 2 tbsp soya cream
5 ml/ 1 tsp of baking powder
1 pinch of salt
170g/ 6 oz self-raising flour
36 cupcake cases
350g/ 12 oz rice milk or dairy free chocolate

Beat the dairy free margarine until soft

Cream the margarine and the sugar together until pale and fluffy

Gradually beat in the eggs

Add the baking powder and the salt to the flour before folding the flour into the mixture

Add the 2 tbsp of soya cream to the mixture

Mix until smooth

Place the cupcake cases into the baking tray/s

Spoon 1 tsp of in to each of the cases

Bake in a preheated oven 180°C/ 350°F/ gas mark 4 for about 20 minutes until lightly golden and springy to the touch

Turn out the cupcakes on to a wire rack to cool

Melt the dairy free rice milk chocolate in a bowl over a saucepan of boiling water on the hob

Allow to cool slightly before spooning over the top of each cupcake ensuring it is completely covered

Leave to cool allowing the topping to set, refrigerate if preferred.

*If preferred the cupcakes can be 18 chocolate and 18 dairy free butter icing; recipe follows.*

**Dairy free Butter Icing**

Makes enough to cover 24 cupcakes/ also enough to fill and cover 1 20cm/ 8 in cake

125g/ 4 oz dairy free margarine
250g/ 8 oz icing sugar sifted
Less milk if you use vanilla extract
5 - 7ml/ 1-1 1/2 tbsp soya milk

Beat the dairy free margarine until soft

Gradually beat in the icing sugar and the soya milk until well blended

Smooth over the cake or pipe on to the cupcakes.

*Above is a photo of the Dairy free chocolate cupcakes I packed for Jacob's Christmas party at Primary school.*

## Apple Swiss Roll

Makes one 20cm/ 8 in roll

100g/ 4 oz plain flour
5 ml/ 1tsp of baking powder
A pinch of salt
225g/. 8 oz caster sugar
3 eggs
5 ml/ 1 tsp of vanilla extract
45ml/ 3 tbsp cold water
Icing sugar, sifted for dusting
100g/ 4 oz apple jam

Mix the flour, baking powder salt and the sugar

Beat in the eggs and vanilla extract until smooth

Stir in the water

Spoon the mixture into a greased and floured 30 x 20 cm/ 12 x 18 in Swiss roll tin (silicon or jelly roll pan)

Bake in a preheated oven at 190°C/ 375°F/ gas mark 5 for 20 minutes until springy to the touch

Sprinkle a clean tea towel with icing sugar and invert the cake on to the towel.

Remove the lining paper, trim the edges and run a knife about 2.5 cm/ 1 in in from the short edge, cutting halfway through the cake.

Roll up the cake from the cut edge before allowing to cool

Once cool unroll the cake and spread with the apple jam almost to the edges.

Roll up again and dust with icing sugar to serve.

**Almond Rice Cake**

Makes one 20cm/ 8 in cake

225g/ 8 oz softened dairy free margarine
225g/ 8 oz caster sugar
3 eggs, beaten
100g/ 4 oz plain flour
75g/ 3 oz self-raising flour
75g/ 3 oz ground rice
2.5 ml/ ½ tsp almond extract

Cream together the dairy free margarine and sugar until light and fluffy

Beat in the eggs a little at a time

Fold in the flours and ground rice then stir in the almond extract.

Spoon into a greased and lined 20 cm/ 8 in cake tin

Bake in a preheated oven at 150°C/ 300°F gas mark 2 for 1 ¼ hours until springy to the touch.

Cool in the tin for 10 minutes before turning out on to a wire rack to finish cooling.

## Orange Gingerbread

Makes one 23 cm/ 9 in cake

450g/ 1lb plain flour
5 ml/ 1tsp ground cinnamon
2.5 ml/ ½ tsp ground ginger
2.5 ml ½ tsp bicarbonate of soda
175g/ 6 oz dairy free margarine
175g/ 6 oz caster sugar
75g/ 3 oz glace orange peel chopped#
Grated rind and juice of ½ large orange
175g/ 6 oz golden syrup, warmed
2 eggs, lightly beaten
A little soya milk

Mix together the flour, spices and the bicarbonate of soda

Rub in the dairy free margarine until the mixture resembles bread crumbs

Stir in the sugar, orange peel and the rind

Make a well in the centre, mix in the orange juice and the warmed syrup

Then stir in the eggs until you have a soft dropping consistency, adding a little of the soya milk if necessary.

Beat well, the spoon into a greased 23 cm/ 9 in square cake tin

Bake in a preheated oven at 160°C/ 325°F/ gas mark 3 for 1 hour until well risen and springy to the touch.

The first photo is one of my favourite memories at my Grandmas' house, totally 80's style and the 70's starter of a prawn cocktail. This photo makes me smile so much and yes, I still make a prawn cocktail at Christmas as well as an alternative.

This photograph was a Sunday teatime at Grandma's, for a birthday. I must confess I cannot remember who's birthday. You can see who inspired my love of baking and even who inspired how I decorate my table for gatherings.

This is my teatime Christmas table from 2018, I definitely see how my Grandma set her table so inspired me. Looking through the photographs I can definitely see how much I am influenced by my Grandmother.

One last Christmas teatime, with some more homemade cupcakes and homemade pie, again I am not sure which year I took this photograph. This beautiful red tablecloth was my Grandma's.

# Marmalade Cake

Makes one 18 cm/ 7 in cake

175g/ 6 oz dairy free margarine
175g/ 6 oz caster sugar
3 eggs, separated
300g/ 10 oz self-raising flour
45 ml/ 3tbsp thick marmalade
50g/ 2 oz chopped mixed candied peel
Grated rind of 1 orange
45 ml/ 3 tbsp water

*For the icing:*
100g/ 4 oz icing sugar sifted
Juice of 1 orange
A few slices of candied orange

Cream together the dairy free margarine and the sugar until light and fluffy

Gradually beat in the egg yolks, then 15 ml/ 1 tbsp of the flour.

Fold in the marmalade, mixed peel, orange rind and water, and then fold in the remaining flour.

Whisk the egg whites until stiff, and then fold them into the mixture using a metal spoon.

Spoon into a greased and lined 18 cm/ 7 in cake tin

Bake in a preheated oven at 180°C/ 350°F/ gas mark 4 for 1 ¼ hours until well risen and springy to the touch.

Leave to cool in the tin for 5 minutes, then turn out on to a wire rack to finish cooling.

To make the icing, place the icing sugar in a bowl and make a well in the centre.

Gradually work enough orange juice to give a spreading consistency.

Spoon over the cake and down the sides and leave to set

Decorate with crystallised orange slices.

## Apple Purée Cake

Makes one 900g/ 2 lb cake

100g/ 4 oz dairy free margarine
225g/ 8 oz soft brown sugar
2 eggs, lightly beaten
225g/ 8 oz plain flour
5 ml/ 1tsp ground cinnamon
2.5 ml/ ½ tsp grated nutmeg
100g/ 4 oz apple sauce
5 ml/ 1tsp bicarbonate of soda
30 ml/ 2 tbsp hot water

Cream together the dairy free margarine and sugar until light and fluffy.

Gradually blend in the eggs

Stir in the flour, cinnamon, nutmeg and apple sauce.

Mix the bicarbonate of soda with the hot water and stir it into the mixture.

Spoon into a greased 900g/ 2 lb loaf tin

Bake in a preheated oven at 180°C/ 350°F/ gas mark 4 for 1¼ hours until a skewer inserted in the centre comes out clean.

## Beetroot Cake

Makes one 20 cm/ 8 in cake

250g/ 9 oz plain flour
15 ml/ 1 tbsp baking powder
5 ml/ 1 tsp ground cinnamon
A pinch of salt
150 ml/ 8 fl oz oil
300g/ 11 oz caster sugar
3 eggs, separated
150g/ 5 oz raw beetroot, peeled and coarsely grated
150g/ 5 oz carrots, coarsely grated
100g/ 4 oz chopped mixed nuts

Mix together the flour, baking powder, cinnamon and salt.

Beat in the oil and the sugar

Beat in the egg yolks, beetroot, carrots and nuts.

Whisk the egg whites until stiff, and then fold into the mixture with a metal spoon.

Spoon the mixture into a greased and lined 20 cm/ 8 in cake tin

Bake in a preheated oven at 180°C/ 350°F/ gas mark 4 for 1 hour until springy to the touch.

**Carrot and Banana Cake**

Makes one 20cm/ 8 in cake

175g/ 6 oz grated carrots
2 bananas mashed
75g/ 3 oz sultanas (golden raisins)
50g/ 2 oz chopped mixed nuts
175g/ 6 oz self-raising flour
5 ml/ 1 tsp baking powder
5 ml/ 1 tsp ground mixed spice
Juice and grated rind of 1 orange
2 eggs, beaten
75g/ 3 oz light muscovado sugar
100 ml/ 3 ½ fl oz sunflower oil

Mix together all of the ingredients until well blended

Spoon into a greased and lined 20 cm/ 8 in cake tin

Bake in a preheated oven at 180°C/ 350°F/ gas mark 4 for 1 hour until a skewer inserted in the centre comes out clean.

## Courgette and Orange Cake

Makes one 25cm/ 10 in cake

225g/ 8 oz dairy free margarine softened
450g/ 1 lb soft brown sugar
4 eggs, lightly beaten
275g/ 10 oz plain flour
15 ml/ 1tbsp baking powder
2.5ml/ ½ tsp salt
5 ml/ 1 tsp ground cinnamon
2.5ml/ ½ tsp grated nutmeg
A pinch of ground cloves
Grated rind and juice of 1 orange
225g/ 8 oz grated courgettes

Cream together the dairy free margarine and sugar until light and fluffy

Gradually beat in the eggs

Fold in the flour, baking powder, salt and the spices alternately with the orange rind and juice

Stir in the courgettes

Spoon into a greased and lined 25cm/ 10 in cake tin

Bake in a preheated oven at 180 °C/ 350°F/ gas mark 4 for 1 hour until golden brown and springy to the touch

If the top begins to over-brown towards the end of baking, cover with grease proof paper/ baking parchment.

**Pumpkin Cake**

Makes one 23 x 33cm/ 9 x 13 in cake

450g/ 1 lb caster sugar
4 eggs, beaten
375ml/ 13 fl oz oil
350g/ 12 oz plain flour
15 ml/ 1 tbsp baking powder
10 ml/ 2 tsp baking soda
10 ml/ 2 tsp ground cinnamon
2.5ml/ ½ tsp ground ginger
A pinch of salt
225g/ 8 oz diced cooked (until soft) pumpkin
100g/ 4 oz walnuts, chopped

Beat together the sugar and eggs until well blended

Beat in the oil

Mix in the remaining ingredients

Spoon into a greased and floured 23 x 33 cm/ 9 x 13 in baking tin

Bake in a preheated oven at 180°c/ 350°F/ gas mark 4 for 1 hour until a skewer inserted in the centre comes out clean.

## Apricot Crunchies

Makes 16

100g/ 4 oz read- to-eat dried apricots
120 ml/ 4 fl oz orange juice
100g/ 4 oz dairy free margarine
75g/ 3 oz wholemeal flour
75g/ 3oz rolled oats
75g/ 3 oz demerara sugar

Soak the apricots in the orange juice for at least 30 minutes until soft, the drain and chop

Rub the dairy free margarine into the flour until the mixture resembles breadcrumbs

Stir in the oats and sugar

Press half of the mixture into a greased 30 x 20cm/ 12 x 8 in Swiss roll tin and sprinkle with the apricots

Spread the remaining mixture on top and press down gently

Bake in a preheated oven at 180°C/ 350°F/ gas mark 4 for 25 minutes until golden brown

Leave to cool in the tin before turning out and cutting into bars

**Nutty Banana Bars**

50g/ 2 oz of dairy free margarine softened
75g/ 3 oz soft brown sugar
2 large bananas, chopped
175g/ 6 oz plain flour
7.5ml/ 1 ½ tsp baking powder
2 eggs, beaten
50g/ 2 oz walnuts roughly chopped

Cream together the dairy free margarine and the sugar

Mash the bananas and stir into the mixture

Mix the flour and baking powder

Add the flour, eggs and nuts to the bananas mixture and beat well

Spoon into a greased and lined 18 x 28cm/ 7 x 11 in cake tin and level the surface

Bake in a preheated oven at 160°C/ 325°F/ gas mark 3 for 30- 35 minutes until springy to the touch

Leave to cool for a few minutes in the tin, then turn out on to a wire rack to finish cooling

Cut into about 14 bars

# 'Butter' Biscuits

Makes 24

100g/ 4 oz dairy free margarine
50g/ 2 oz caster sugar
Grated rind of 1 lemon
150g/ 5 oz self raising flour

Cream together the dairy free margarine and the sugar until light and fluffy

Work in the lemon rind, and then mix in the flour to stiff mixture

Shape into walnut sized balls and arrange well apart on a greased baking sheet, then press down lightly with a fork to flatten

Bake the biscuits in a preheated oven at 180°C/ 350°F/ gas mark 4 for 15 minutes until golden brown.

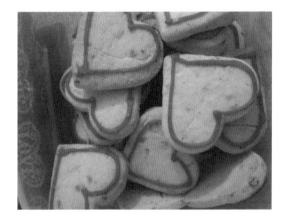

*The heart shaped cookies to the left are the butter biscuit or short bread recipe, however I made them for my hubby, and I added freeze dried raspberries.*

*These dairy free butter biscuits I made for a Halloween party. The bat cookies were vanilla and iced with purple icing and the pumpkin cookies were orange flavour and decorated with orange icing.*

## Crisp Nut Biscuits

Makes 30

100g/ 4 oz soft brown sugar
1 egg, beaten
5 ml/ 1 tsp vanilla extract
45 ml/ 3 tbsp plain flour
100g/ 4 oz chopped mixed nuts

Beat the sugar with the eggs and the vanilla extract

Blend in the flour and the nuts

Place small spoonfuls on a greased and floured baking sheet and flatten slightly with a fork

Bake the biscuits in a preheated oven at 190°C/ 375°F/ gas mark 5 for 10 minutes

## Country Wholemeal Bread

Makes two 450g/ 1 lb loaves

20 ml/ 4 tsp dried yeast
5 ml/ 1 tsp caster sugar
600 ml/ 1 pt warm water
25g/ 1 oz/ 2 tbsp vegetable fat
800g/ 1 ¾ lb wholemeal flour
10 ml/ 2 tsp salt
10 ml/ 2 tsp malt extract
1 egg, beaten
25g/ 1 oz cracked wheat

Blend the yeast with the sugar and a little of the warm water and leave for 20 minutes until frothy

Rub the fat into the floor, salt and malt extract and make a well in the centre

Stir in the yeast mixture and the remaining warm water and mix into a soft dough

Knead well until elastic and no longer sticky

Place in an oiled bowl, cover with oiled clingfilm and leave in a warm place for about 1 hour until doubled in size

Knead the dough again and shape into two greased 450g/ 1 lb loaf tins

Leave to rise in a warm place for about 40 minutes until the dough rises just above the top of the tins

Brush the tops of the loaves generously with egg and sprinkle with cracked wheat

Bake in a preheated oven at 230°C/ 450°F/ gas mark 8 for about 30 minutes until golden brown and hollow sounding when tapped on the base.

*The photograph above is loaves I made of wholemeal bread and white bread; both of these delicious loaves are dairy free.*

*The picture to the left is soft white bread rolls I made from the dough for the dairy free white bread.*

*In the past I made quite a bit of bread by hand as most store-bought bread had milk powder listed in the ingredients, however not as much now but little man does have his favourites.*

**Cranberry Bread**

Makes one 450g/ 1 lb loaf

225g/ 8 oz plain flour
2.5ml/ ½ tsp salt
2.5ml ½ baking soda
225/ 8 oz caster sugar
7.5ml/ 1 ½ baking powder
Juice and grated rind of 1 orange
1 egg, beaten
25g/ 1 oz lard melted
100g/ 4 oz fresh or frozen cranberries crushed
50g/ 2 oz walnuts, coarsely chopped

Mix together the dry ingredients in a large bowl

Put the orange juice and rind in a measuring jug and make up to 175ml/ 6 fl oz with water

Stir into the dry ingredients with the egg and the lard

Stir in the cranberries and nuts

Spoon into a greased 450g/ 1 lb loaf tin

Bake in a preheated oven at 160°C/ 325°F/ gas mark 3 for about an hour until a skewer inserted into the centre comes out clean, then keep for 24 hours before cutting.

## Pumpkin Bread

Makes three 450g/ 1 lb loaves

275g/ 10 oz wholemeal flour
225g/ 8 oz plain flour
225g/ 8 ox muscovado sugar
100g/ 4 oz chopped mixed nuts
15 ml/ 1 tbsp baking soda
5 ml/ 1tsp salt
5 ml/ 1 tsp ground cinnamon
2.5 ml/ ½ tsp grated nutmeg
225g/ 8 oz stoned dates, chopped
675g/ 1 ½ lb cooked pumpkin purée
250 ml/ 8 fl oz clear honey
250 ml/ 8 fl oz oil

Mix together the flours, sugar, nuts, baking soda, salt cinnamon and nutmeg

Stir in the dates

Blend together the pumpkin, honey and oil then stir into the dry ingredients and mix well

Shape the mixture into three greased 450g/ 1 lb loaf tins

Bake in a preheated oven at 180°C/ 350°F/ gas mark 4 for about 1 hour until a skewer inserted into the centre comes out clean.

## Sun-dried Tomato Bread

Makes one 900g/ 2 lb loaf

15g/ ½ oz fresh yeast
5 ml/ 1tsp caster sugar
300 ml/ ½ pint warm water
550g/ 1 ¼ lb strong plain bread flour
A pinch of salt
50g/ 2 oz of tomato purée
50g/ 2 oz sun-dried tomatoes in oil, drained and chopped

Blend the yeast with the sugar and a little of the warm water and leave until frothy

Place the flour and salt in a bowl and make a well in the centre

Mix the tomato purée and the remaining water and stir into the flour and yeast mixture and mix to a firm dough

Knead until elastic and no longer sticky

Place in an oiled bowl and cover with clingfilm

Leave for 1 hour until doubled in size

Knead again lightly and work in the sun-dried tomatoes

Shape into a 900g/ 2 lb loaf tin. Cover and leave in a warm place for 35 minutes until the dough has risen above the top of the tin

Bake in a preheated oven at 400°C/ 200°F/ gas mark 6 for 30 minutes until golden and hollow sounding when tapped on the base.

**Turnip Bread**

Makes one 450g/ 1 lb loaf tin

100g/ 4 oz strong plain flour
100g/ 4 oz caster sugar
2.5ml/ ½ tsp baking soda
2.5ml/ ½ tsp baking powder
5ml/ 1 tsp ground allspice
A pinch of salt
1 egg, lightly beaten
100g/ 4 oz cooked turnip pure
60ml/ 4 tbsp oil

Mix together the dry ingredients and make a well in the centre

Blend together the egg, turnip and oil, then mix into the dry ingredients until well blended

Spoon into a greased and lined 450g/ 1 lb loaf tin

Bake in a preheated oven at 180°C/ 350°F/ gas mark 4 for 1 hour until a skewer inserted into the centre comes out clean

## Amy's Oat Crunchies

*A dear friend who enjoys cooking gave me this recipe soon after Jacob was diagnosed with the allergy.*

170g/ 6 oz rolled oats
100g/ 4 oz soft brown sugar
1 egg, lightly beaten
125 ml/ 4 fl oz sunflower oil

Blend all the ingredients well

Using a tsp put walnut sized blobs on a greased baking sheet

Bake in a preheated oven at 160°C/ 325 ° F/ gas marks 3 for about 20 minutes until lightly golden

Leave in the tin to cool slightly before turning out on to a wire rack to cool

*The photo above is of the lovely day out we had at a nature park going for a walk and we had a picnic, it what a lovely day. I as always made sure to pack a lunch for Jacob suitable for his diet, however Amy had made a few extras that he could have, and I was so happy.*

# Mummy's Milk Free Lollies

*For use with a small six lolly freezer suitable container*

½ a large or 1 small banana
45 ml/ 3 tbsp honey
300ml Soya milk

Crush the banana in a glass jug or container used with a hand blender

Add the honey to the banana and mix with a fork

Blend in the 300ml of milk a hand blender does this well as the liquid thickens like the consistency of a smooth.

Poor the mixture into the moulds and refrigerate for 2-3 hours.

Once the lollies are frozen they are ready to eat, to loosen each individual lolly from the mould half immerse the container in warm water for a few seconds then the lollies should slide out easily when pulled gently by the handle.

*The photograph's above are of Jacob enjoying his first dairy free ice lolly, he was pretending to be shy, bless him.*

# Beef and Vegetable Salad with Peanuts

500g/ 1 lb cubed beef (sirloin or chopped fillet)
1 tbsp oil
250g/ 8 oz carrots cut into match sticks
250g/ 8 oz green beans, trimmed
200g/ 7 oz broccoli florets
2 spring onions, finely chopped

For the dressing:
6 tbsp lemon juice
6 tbsp sunflower oil
1 tsp sesame oil
1 tsp can sugar
1 tsp ginger finely chopped
1 clove garlic finely chopped
Salt and freshly ground pepper

In addition:
100g/ 4 oz roasted peanuts

Preheat the oven to 160ºC/ 325ºF/ gas mark 4

Trim the beef

Heat the oil and brown the meat on all sides and then put it into the oven and roast for about 20 minutes

Take the meat out and wrap in aluminium foil and let rest in the oven on a very low heat

Blanch the carrots in boiling salted water for 4 minutes, when each vegetable has been blanched, take out the pan, refresh in cold water and drain

Blanch the broccoli florets in boiling salted water for 4 minutes

Blanch the green beans in boiling salted water for 8 minutes

For the dressing, mix all the dressing ingredients and season to taste

Mix the prepared salad ingredients with half of the dressing.  Slice the beef thinly across the grain and mix lightly with the salad

Arrange on a large platter, sprinkle with the rest of the dressing and scatter with the peanuts.

## Dads' Chickpea and Spinach Salad

4 tbsp olive oil
2 tbsp cider vinegar
1 tsp English mustard
1 pinch of sugar
Salt and freshly ground pepper to taste
350g/ 12 oz baby spinach leaves
400g/ 14 oz canned chickpeas, rinsed and drained
2 beefsteak tomatoes, cores, seeded and diced
1 ripe avocado, pitted and diced
8 plums, pitted and cut into wedges
3 spring onions, finely chopped

Whisk together the oil, vinegar, mustard and sugar in a large bowl to make vinaigrette.  Season with salt and pepper

Add the spinach, chickpeas, tomatoes, avocado, plums and spring onions and then toss gently to coat in the vinaigrette

Divide between four plates and serve

# Chicken with Bacon and Potato and water cress Salad

For the potato salad:
800g/ 1 ¾ lb new potatoes, peeled and halved if large
2 tbsp walnut oil
4 tbsp vegetable oil
3 tbsp cider vinegar
1 tsp English mustard
Salt and freshly ground pepper to taste
4 spring onions

For the chicken:
4 skinless boneless chicken breast, halved lengthwise, or three chicken breast fillets
and a Quorn chicken fillet for my vegetarian hubby.
Salt and freshly ground pepper, to taste
1 tbsp olive oil
1 tsp dairy free margarine
4 slices of bacon
2 vegetarian chorizo sausages
1 tbsp finely chopped fresh parsley
1 bunch watercress, trimmed
3- 4 lettuce leaves, torn into bite-size pieces

Cook the potatoes in boiling salted water until tender, about 25 minutes.  Drain and cut into bite-size pieces

Whisk the oils, vinegar, mustard, salt and pepper in a large bowl.  Add the potatoes and spring onions, mix well and let stand to absorb the flavours

Meanwhile, heat the grill and season the Quorn chicken with salt and pepper.  Put under the grill and cook thoroughly; this will cook slightly faster than the chicken

Then season the chicken with salt and pepper and cook under the grill after the Quorn chicken

Heat the oil and dairy free margarine in a skillet and fry the meat free chorizo until soft and piping hot all the way through

Then without wiping the pan fry the bacon until crisp

Take out and drain on paper towels, leaving the fat to be disposed of

Arrange the potato salad on plates with the watercress and lettuce, add the chicken, the Quorn chicken and then the chorizo to hubby's and the bacon to the rest and serve.

**Chicken on stir-fried Vegetables**


5 ml/ 1 tsp Chinese five-spice powder
2 limes
180 ml/ 12 tbsp dark soy sauce
4 chicken breast fillets or 3 chicken breast fillets and a Quorn fillet for vegetarian hubby
300g/ 11 oz mange tout trimmed
1 medium sized courgette sliced
200g/ 7 oz carrots, peeled and cut into match sticks
30 ml/ 2 tbsp oil
2.5 ml/ ½ tsp chilli powder
Salt
100 ml/ 3 fl oz vegetable stock
100g/ 4 oz bean sprouts
2 tbsp/ 30ml toasted sesame seeds


Wash the limes, remove the zest and chop finely and squeeze the juice

Mix the five-spice powder, the zest and the juice of the limes, and 6- 8 tbsp of soy sauce to make a marinade

Marinate the chicken and the Quorn chicken fillet for about 15 minutes

Grill the Quorn chicken under a medium heat until cooked through, 3-5 minutes on each side depending on the thickness and follow with the chicken breast fillets

Heat the oil in a wok, add the mange tout and stir fry for 1 minute

Add the courgettes and carrots and cook for a further 2 minutes, then ad the chilli powder, 2 tbsp/ 60 ml of soy sauce and salt. Then add the vegetable stock and cook for a further 5 minutes.

Slice the chicken and drizzle the remaining soy sauce, or to taste. Serve the stir fried vegetables on to plates and put the chicken and Quorn chicken on top.

## Carrot and Tuna Salad

500g/ 1 lb carrots, peeled and coarsely grated
200g/ 6 oz can of water-packed tuna
180 ml/ 6 tbsp olive oil
120 ml/ 4 tbsp white wine vinegar
60 ml/ 2 tbsp coarse Dijon mustard
2 tsp/ 10ml green peppercorns
90- 120 ml/ 3- 4 tbsp lemon juice
Lemon wedges to garnish
Coriander to garnish

Drain and flake the tuna

Mix the tuna with the carrots and put on to plates

For the dressing, put the vinegar, lemon juice and the Dijon mustard into a bowl and blend in the oil adding in trickles

Finally mix in the peppercorns and sprinkle the dressing over the salad

Serve garnished with lemon wedges and coriander

# Moroccan Lamb Kebabs with Alpro Soya Yoghurt Sauce

300g/ 12 oz/ 1 lb lamb, from the leg
80g/ 3 oz mixed salad leaves
4 pita breads
1 lemon
8 wooden skewers

For the marinade:
Juice of 1 lemon
50 ml/ 2 tbsp olive oil
50 lm/ 2 tbsp chilli oil
2 sprigs rosemary, roughly chopped
1 tbsp/ 30 ml ginger paste
1 pinch cumin

For the yoghurt Sauce:
100g/4 oz fresh mint, roughly chopped
400g/ 14 oz Alpro soya natural style yoghurt
1 tsp/ 5 ml lemon zest
Pinch of fine caster sugar


Mix all the marinade ingredients and put into a freezer bag

Cut the meat into ¾ in/ 2 cm cubes and put into the freezer bag with the marinade

Seal and knead to make sure the meat is coated in the marinade, put into the refrigerator and leave for at least 2 hours.

Soak the wooden skewers in enough water to cover for 30 minutes to prevent burning

For the yoghurt sauce put the yoghurt into a bowl and then mix through the mint and the lemon zest and a punch of caster sugar. Then chill in the refrigerator

Preheat the grill, take the meat out of the marinade and thread on the wooden skewers. Grill on all sides for 5 minutes, 20 minutes in full

Meanwhile, fold the pita breads and briefly toast/ warm them and cut the lemon into 8 wedges

Arrange the kebabs on plates with the pita bread. Garnish with the salad and sprinkle with yoghurt sauce. The remaining sauce can be served separately.

## Spaghetti with Grilled Vegetables

400g/ 14 oz spaghetti
600g/ 1 ¼ lb tomatoes
1 clove garlic finely chopped
Olive oil
1 dash of red wine
1 tbsp/ 30 ml sesame seeds
Salt and freshly milled pepper
1 aubergine sliced
1 green courgette, sliced
1 yellow courgette, sliced
1 tsp dried thyme
3 tbsp mozzarella style sheeze (vegan cheese)
Rosemary, to garnish


Cook the spaghetti according to the package instructions until al dente

Meanwhile drop the tomatoes into boiling water for a few seconds, refresh in cold water, then skin, quarter, deseed and chop

Heat 2 tablespoons oil and sauté the garlic, then add a little red wine and the chopped tomatoes

Remove from the heat, add the sesame seeds, and season to taste with the salt and pepper

Sprinkle the aubergine and courgette with olive oil and thyme and season with salt and pepper.  Put on a grill and cook for 1- 2 minutes each side.

Drain the spaghetti, mix with the tomatoes and put into warmed bowls

Add a slice of each vegetable and sprinkle with 1 tbsp mozzarella style sheeze.  Serve garnished with rosemary.

Sprinkle the rest 0f the vegetables with the remaining mozzarella style sheeze and serve separately.

# Butternut Squash and Sweet Potato Soup

1 tbsp olive oil
1 medium onion, peeled and diced
2 cloves garlic, peeled and crushed
1 tsp hot curry powder
300g/11oz sweet potato, peeled weight and diced
250g/ 9 oz butternut squash, peeled weight and diced
½/ tsp/ 2.5 ml salt
2 tbsp basil leaves, torn
750ml, 1¼pts vegetable stock (2 stock cubes)
250ml/ 9 fl oz dairy free soya cream

Heat oil in large saucepan, add onion and garlic, cook until soft, add curry powder and cook a further minute.

Add sweet potato and butternut squash, stir and cook for 2 minutes

Add salt, basil leaves, stock, bring to the boil and reduce to a simmer for 20 minutes or until the sweet potato is cooked, ten very near the end add the soya single cream

Blend or process vegetable mixture until smooth.

Serve soup hot or cold with chopped basil or chives.

*Delicious butternut squash and sweet potato soup, so warming and tasty with the chives.*

## Peas and fresh Tuna

120 ml/ 4 tbsp olive oil
1 onion, peeled and thinly sliced
1 garlic clove peeled and crushed
4 tuna steaks, about 150- 200g/ 5 ½- 7 oz each
Salt and pepper
180ml/ 5 tbsp white wine
2 tsp tomato purée
2.5 ml/ ½ tsp caster sugar
250g/ 9 oz cooked peas
15 ml/ 3 tsp chopped parsley, to garnish
Tuna steaks

Heat the oil in a large frying pan over a medium heat

Fry the onion and garlic together for about 5 minutes, until slightly browned, remove from the pan and set aside

In the same pan fry the seasoned tuna steaks on both sides for 3 minutes, until lightly browned

Return the cooked onions and garlic to the pan

Mix the wine, tomato purée and sugar together, and pour over the tuna, cooked onions and garlic

Cover the pan and cook over a very low heat for 10 minutes

Add the peas, season and heat through for a few minutes

Garnish with parsley and serve

**New Potato and Red onion Salad (Jersey Royals)**

675g/ 1 ½ lb new potatoes scrubbed
Salt and pepper
90 ml/ 3 tbsp olive oil
30 ml/ 1 tbsp white wine vinegar
2 spring onions, thinly sliced
1 red onion, peeled and thinly sliced
175ml/ 6 fl oz real (dairy free) mayonnaise
90 ml/ 3 tbsp chopped chives

Cook the potatoes in boiling salted water for 10- 15 minutes, until tender

Blend together the oil and the vinegar

Drain the potatoes thoroughly and place in a large bowl

Add the oil and vinegar mixture and the sliced onions, season and put the bowl aside to cool

Once the potato mixture is cool, add the mayonnaise and chives and mix thoroughly

Chill before serving

## Oat and Apricot Fruit Cake

175g/ 6 oz Vitalite dairy free margarine softened
50g/ 2 oz soft brown sugar
30 ml/ 2 tbsp clear honey
3 eggs, beaten
175g/ 6 oz whole meal flour
50g/ 2 oz of oat flour
10 ml/ 2 tsp baking powder
250g/ 9 oz dried mixed fruit
50g/ 2 oz ready to eat dried apricots, chopped
Grated rind and juice of 1 lemon

Cream the Vitalite and the sugar with the honey until light and fluffy

Gradually beat in the eggs, alternately with the flours and baking powder

Stir in the dries fruit

Stir in the lemon juice and rind

Spoon into a greased and lined 20cm/ 8-inch cake tin

Bake in a preheated oven at 180 ºC/ 325 ºF, gas mark 4 for 1 hour

Then reduce the heat in the oven to 160 ºC/ 325 ºF or gas mark 3 and bake for a further 30 minutes until a skewer into the centre comes out clean

Cover the top with baking paper if the cake begins to brown to quickly

**Aubergine dip with flatbreads**


1 large aubergine
4 tbsp extra virgin olive oil
1 tsp ground cumin
150 ml ALPRO Greek style plain yogurt
1 small garlic clove, crushed
2 tbsp chopped fresh coriander
1 tbsp lemon juice
4 flour tortillas
Salt and black pepper


Slice the aubergine lengthways into 5mm thick slices

Mix 3 tbsp of the olive oil with the cumin and salt and pepper and brush over the aubergine slices

Cook under a grill for 4- 5 minutes on each side until charred and tender

Leave to cool and then finely chop

Mix the aubergine and ALPRO yogurt in a bowl and then stir in the garlic, coriander and lemon juice then the remaining olive oil and salt and pepper to taste and transfer to a serving bowl

Cook the tortillas for 3 minutes on each side under the grill until toasted, cut into triangles and then serve immediately

*I decided to try this dip for a movie night once because I love onion and garlic dip with tortillas or crisps, however a lot of them you buy contain dairy. Hubby can have this too as it is vegetarian friendly.*

# Bean, lemon and rosemary hummus

6 tbsp extra virgin olive oil, plus a little extra to serve
4 shallots, finely chopped
2 large garlic cloves, crushed
1 tsp chopped rosemary, plus extra sprigs to garnish
Grated rind and juice of ½ lemon
2x 400g cans of butter beans
Salt and black pepper
Toasted ciabatta to serve

Heat the oil in a frying pan, add the shallots, garlic, chopped rosemary and lemon rind

Cook over a low heat, stir occasionally for 10 minutes until the shallots are softened then leave to cool

Transfer the shallot mixture to a food processor, add the remining ingredients and process until smooth

Spread the hummus on to toasted ciabatta

Garnish with the rosemary sprigs and a drizzle of extra virgin olive oil

## Baked eggs with tomato

100g or 3 ½ oz cherry tomatoes, halved
1 shallot diced
1 clove of garlic, minced
2 tbsp olive oil
2 large free-range eggs
Handful of chopped basil

Preheat the oven to 180°C or gas mark 4

Combine the garlic, shallot, oil and tomatoes in a bowl

Season with salt and black pepper and toss to combine

Spoon the mixture into ramekins

Carefully break an egg over the top

Bake in the hot oven for 8- 10 minutes, until the egg white is set

Remove from the oven and scatter over the fresh basil and a little more cracked black pepper and serve.

# Salmon and vegetable bake

4 thick salmon steaks
350g or 12 oz of broccoli broken into small florets
400g or 14 oz of baby sprouts
12 cherry tomatoes
4 small shallots cut into wedges
1 lemon
3 sprigs of rosemary
100ml or 3 ¼ fl. oz olive oil
2 tbsp fresh thyme, chopped
½ tsp of mixed peppercorns, crushed

Preheat the oven to 200°C or gas mark 6

Arrange the salmon steaks in a baking dish

Surround with the broccoli, sprouts, tomatoes and shallots

Cut 4 slices of lemon from the first lemon ad chop the slices in half to garnish the salmon, with the rosemary

Squeeze the rest of the lemon into a jug, then whisk in the oil, thyme, peppercorns and a little salt

Then drizzle the mixture over the salmon and the vegetables

Bake for 25 minutes until the fish is just cooked and the vegetables are just tender

**Vegan chilli**

2 tbsp olive oil
1 onion, finely chopped
2 cloves of garlic, crushed
½ tsp cayenne pepper
450g veggie Quorn mince
400g or 14 oz of tinned tomatoes, chopped
200 ml or 7 fl oz vegetable stock
400g or 14 oz of tinned mixed beans, drained
200g or 7 oz of tinned sweetcorn, drained
200g grated Oak smoked vegan Sheese
2 tbsp coriander, chopped
Lime wedges and tortilla chips to serve

Heat the oil in a large saucepan and fry the onion stirring occasionally

Add the garlic and the cayenne pepper and cook for two minutes

Then add the Quorn mince

Fry the mince until it starts to brown

Then add the chopped tomatoes, vegetable stock, beans and sweetcorn then bring to a gentle simmer

Cook for 30 minutes, stirring occasionally until the mice is tender and the sauce has thickened a little

Season to taste with salt and pepper, divide the chilli between warm bowls and sprinkle on the cheese and the coriander, then serve with lime wedges and tortilla chips on the side.

## Onion, tomato and chickpea soup

2 tbsp olive oil
2 red onions, roughly chopped
2 garlic cloves, finely chopped
2 tsp brown sugar
625g or 1 ¼ lb tomatoes, skinned and roughly chopped
2 tsp of harissa paste
3 tsp tomato paste
400g or 14 oz can of chickpeas, drained and rinsed
900ml or 1 ½ pints of vegetable stock
Salt and pepper

Heat the oil in a large saucepan, then add the red onion and fry over a low heat for 10 minutes, stirring occasionally until, the edges have began to brown

Then stir in the garlic and the sugar, then cook for 10 more minutes, stirring frequently as the onions begin to caramelize

Stir in the tomatoes and harissa paste and fry for 5 minutes

Mix in the tomato puree, chickpeas, stock and salt and pepper

Cover and simmer for 45 minutes until the tomatoes and onions are very soft

Taste and adjust the seasoning if needed

Serve, it tastes amazing with ciabata bread

*The soup is so heart- warming and delicious, it feeds a family really well. I have also served it with tiger bread as well, because Jacob loves it and from ALDI is dairy free and not expensive.*

**Butternut soup with peanut pesto**


Soup
2 tbsp olive oil
1 onion, finely chopped
1 butternut squash, about 750g or 1 ½ lb peeled and deseeded, cut into chunks
400g or 14 oz can of coconut milk
1 tbsp of vegan Thai green curry paste
600 ml or 1 pint of vegetable stock

Pesto
1 green chilli, deseeded and finely chopped
2 tbsp unsalted peanuts, roughly chopped
4 tbsp chopped coriander
1 cm or ½ inch piece of fresh root ginger, peeled and grated
1 tbsp olive oil
Salt and pepper


Mix all the ingredients for the pesto together I n a small serving bowl and season with a little salt and pepper then set aside

Heat the oil in a large saucepan, then add the onion and butternut squash and cook over a medium to high heat for 5-6 minutes

Once the squash is golden in places add the coconut milk, curry paste and the vegetable stock and bring to the boil

Then cover and simmer gently for 30 minutes until the squash is tender

Transfer the soup in batches, to a food processor and blend until smooth, or blend with a hand blender

Then return to the pan and reheat, then serve with a swirl of the pesto

# Mushroom Bolognese

25g or 1 oz dried wild mushrooms such as porcini and chanterelle
2 tbsp olive oil
1 large onion, chopped
1 celery stick, finely chopped
1 carrot, finely chopped
2 garlic cloves, crushed
500g or 1 lb 2 oz mixed mushrooms, trimmed and roughly chopped
150ml or ¼ pint red wine
400g or 14 oz can chopped tomatoes
1 tbsp tomato puree
1 tsp balsamic vinegar
2 tsp dried oregano
300g or 10 oz dried spaghetti
Salt and pepper
Grated vegan Sheese to serve

Place the dried mushrooms in a bowl and pour over enough hot water to cover, then allow to soak for 20 minutes

Heat the oil in a large saucepan, add the onion, celery, carrot and garlic then cook over a low heat for 8 minutes, stirring occasionally until softened

Then turn up the heat and stir in the fresh mushrooms and cook for 3 or 4 minutes

Then strain the soaked dried mushrooms through a sieve, reserving the liquid

Then add the dried mushrooms to the pan

Pour over the wine, bring to the boil and cook until reduced by half, then stir in the reserved soaking liquid

Stir in the tomatoes, tomato puree, vinegar, oregano, then season with the salt and pepper and bring to the boil

Reduce the heat, cover and simmer for 40- 50 minutes until the sauce is thick and the mushrooms are tender

Meanwhile, cook the spaghetti in a large saucepan of lightly salted boiling water for 8- 10 minutes, or according to the packet instructions until al dente

Drain and serve straight away topped with the mushroom sauce and grated sheese

# Gnocchi in tomato and leek sauce

Gnocchi
625g or 1 ¼ floury potatoes such as king Edwards or Maris Piper, scrubbed
125g or 4 oz plain flour
Salt and pepper

Sauce
1 tbsp olive oil
1 leek cleaned, trimmed and chopped
1 garlic clove, crushed
4 ripe tomatoes roughly chopped
1 tbsp tomato puree
Pinch of sugar
Small handful of torn basil leaves
Salt and pepper

Cook the potatoes in their skins in a large saucepan of salted boiling water for about 20 minutes until tender

Drain and leave long enough for them to be cool enough to handle but not cold

To make the sauce, heat the oil in a frying pan and add the leek, cook over a medium heat for 5 minutes until tender

Then add the garlic and the tomatoes and cook for a further 5 minutes, until the tomatoes are soft

Stir in the tomato puree and add a little water to make a sauce

Then add the sugar, season with salt and pepper and simmer for 3 minutes

Peel the potatoes and mash them or pass them through a potato ricer until smooth

Season with salt and pepper, then knead in the flour to form a dough

Divide the gnocchi dough into four pieces and roll each piece into a thick sausage

Cut into 1.5 cm or ¾ inch pieces and press with the prongs of a fork to mark a ridged pattern

Cook the gnocchi in a large saucepan of salted boiling water for 1- 2 minutes until they float to the surface

Then remove from the pan with a slotted spoon and add to the sauce

Then add the basil and gently turn the gnocchi to coat in the sauce and serve with an extra grinding of pepper

## Pearl barley risotto with carrots

225g or 7 ½ oz pearl barley
400g or 14 oz baby carrots, scrubbed
5 tbsp olive oil
1 large onion, finely chopped
1 large leek, trimmed, cleaned and thinly sliced
1 garlic clove, thinly sliced
1 tbsp thyme leaves
1 tsp ground coriander
1.2 litres or 2 pints of vegetable stock, plus extra if needed
2 tbsp of chopped flat leaf parsley to garnish
Salt and pepper


Put the pearl barley in a bowl, pour over enough boiling water to cover and leave to stand for 10 minutes

Toss the carrots in a shallow roasting tin with 2 tbsp of the oil until evenly coated

Then roast in a preheated oven at 200°C or 400°F or gas mark 6, for 20 minutes until tender and lightly charred in places

Heat the remaining oil in a frying pan, then add the onion and the leek with the garlic and thyme and cook over a medium heat, stirring occasionally, for 4 minutes until soft and pale golden

Stir in the ground coriander and cook for a further a further 1 minute

Drain the pearl barley and add to the frying pan with half of the vegetable stock and bring to the boil

Cover and simmer very gently, stirring occasionally, for about 10 minutes until almost all of the stock is absorbed

Add the remaining stock and stir, then cover and simmer gently again until the pearl barley is tender and so me of the stock is still left in the pan, adding more stock if necessary

Add the roasted carrots to the risotto and stir through

Season, garnish with the parsley and serve, it tastes great with warm wholemeal bread

# Spinach and mushroom lasagne

4 tbsp dairy free spread such as Vitalite
2 onions, chopped
2 sticks celery, chopped
625g or 1 ¼ lb mushrooms, roughly chopped
3 garlic cloves, crushed
2 tsp dried thyme or oregano
150ml or ¼ pint red wine
3 tbsp sun- dried tomato puree
450g or 1lb spinach, washed and dried
4 tbsp plain flour
600ml or 1 pint almond milk
200g or 7 oz lasagne sheets
100g or 3 ½ oz Sheese vegan style cheese, grated
Salt and pepper

Melt 1 tbsp of the dairy free margarine in a large frying pan, then fry the onions and celery for 5 minutes

Add the mushrooms and fry for a further 10 minutes, until the mushrooms are lightly browned, and all the liquid has evaporated

Stir in the garlic, herbs and red wine and cook for a couple of minutes

Stir in the tomato paste

Then gradually add the spinach, turning it in the hot sauce until it has wilted

Season to taste with salt and pepper

Melt the remaining dairy free spread in a saucepan, then add the flour and cook for 1 minute

Gradually blend in the milk, stirring well to remove any lumps

Cook for 3- 4 minutes until thickened

To assemble, spoon a quarter of the mushroom sauce in a shallow oven proof dish and spread level

Arrange a single layer of lasagne sheets on top, snapping the sheets to fit where necessary

Drizzle about a third of the white sauce, then spoon another quarter of the mushroom sauce into the dish and arrange more lasagne sheets on top

Repeat with another layer of mushroom sauce and lasagne sheets then spread with remaining mushroom sauce, then the white sauce and sprinkle with vegan sheese

Bake in a preheated oven, 180°C or 350°F or gas mark 4 for about 50- 60 minutes until the surface is bubbling and lightly golden

Leave to stand for 10 minutes before serving

**Daddy's apple and walnut roast**


3 tbsp olive oil
1 large fennel bulb chopped
200g or 7 oz of walnuts roughly chopped
3 garlic cloves chopped
75g or 3 oz white or brown bread, torn into pieces
1 crisp dessert apple
15g ½ oz coriander chopped
1 tsp ground paprika
2 tsp caster sugar
4 tbsp tomato ketchup
2 tbsp balsamic vinegar
Salt


Line a 900ml loaf tin with baking paper, pushing the paper into the corners

Heat the oil in a frying pan and fry the fennel for 5 minutes

Then add the walnuts and the garlic and fry for a further 2 minutes

Put the bread in a food processor and blend to make coarse breadcrumbs

Tip in the walnut mixture and blend until the nuts are finely chopped

Peel, core and grate the apple into the mixture

Add the coriander, paprika, sugar and a little salt and blend very briefly to mix

Pack firmly into the tin and level the surface, then bake in a preheated oven at 180°c or gas mark 4 for 30 minutes

Lift out of the tin, peel away the sides of the paper and return to the oven for a further 10 minutes

Then leave to stand for a further 10 minutes

Mix together the ketchup and balsamic vinegar in a small bowl, then thickly slice the nut roast and serve with the sauce

**Toasted potato bread with tomatoes**

Bread
or 13 oz potatoes, peeled and cut into chunks
1 tsp of fast- action dries yeast
1 tsp caster sugar
1 tbsp sunflower oil, plus extra for oiling
200g or 7 oz strong white bread flour, plus extra for dusting
100g or 3 ½ oz od strong wholemeal bread flour
2 tbsp chopped rosemary
1 tbsp thyme leaves
Salt and pepper

Topping
2 tbsp olive oil
250g or 8 oz cherry tomatoes, in mixed colours, halved
½ tsp thyme leaves
½ tsp sea salt flakes

Cook the potato chunks in a large saucepan of lightly salted boiling water for 15- 20 minutes, until tender but not mushy

Drain well, reserving the cooking liquid

Put 6 tbsp of the cooking liquid into a large bowl and leave to cool until lukewarm

Sprinkle over the yeast and then stir in the sugar and set aside for 10 minutes

Mash the potatoes with the oil, then stir in the yeast mixture and mix well with a wooden spoon

Mix in the flours, herbs and salt and pepper, then turn out on to a lightly floured surface and knead well to incorporate the last of the floor

Knead the dough until soft and pliable, then put into a lightly oiled bowl, cover with clingfilm and leave to rise in a warm place for 1 hour until well risen

Knead the dough on a lightly floured surface, then roughly shape it into a round, then place in on a baking tray and cover it with oiled clingfilm

Leave it to prove for a further 30 minutes

Score a cross into the dough with a sharp knife

Bake in a preheated oven at 220°C or 425°F or gas mark 7, for 35- 40 minutes until well risen and crusty on top

Then transfer to a wire rack to cool for 30 minutes

Cut 4 slices of the bread and lightly toast it

Heat the remainder of the oil for a frying pan

Add the tomatoes and cook over a high heat for 2- 3 minutes until softened

Then stir in the sea salt flakes and the thyme

Then serve on the toasted bread, seasoned with pepper

**Nana's plum, banana and apple crumbles**


Fruit filling
6 plums halved and pitted
50g or 2 oz of dairy free margarine such as Vitalite
2 dessert apples, peeled, cored and cut into chunks
2 tbsp demerara sugar
2 bananas cut into chunks
½ tsp ground cinnamon
Pinch of ground allspice

Crumble
100g or 3 ½ oz plain flour
50g or 2 oz of Vitalite, cubed
4 tbsp demerara sugar
4 tbsp rolled oats


Cook the plums with the Vitalite in a saucepan over a gentle heat for 3 minutes

Add the apples and the demerara sugar and cook, stirring occasionally, for a further 2-3 minutes

Remove the pan from the heat, then add the bananas and spices and then toss gently to coat all the fruit in the sugar and spices

Then divide the mixture between 4 x 250 ml or 8 fl oz ramekins

Put the flour for the crumble in a bowl, add the Vitalite and rub in with fingertips until the mixture resembles breadcrumbs

Then stir in the sugar and the rolled oats

Spoon evenly over the top of the fruit in each dish , place on a baking tray and bake in a preheated oven at 200°C or 400°F or gas mark 6, for 20 minutes until the crumble is golden and the fruit is bubbling

Serve with vanilla soya yoghurt

The photograph above is the same recipe that Jacob's Nana makes, she uses a large roasting dish rather than ramekins but it is so delicious.

## Apricot and papaya fool

150g or 5 oz ready to eat, dried apricots, chopped
25g or 1 oz dried papaya, chopped
450ml or ¾ pint sweetened soya milk
2 tbsp flax seed oil
4 strawberries to decorate

Soak the dried apricots and papaya in the sweetened soya milk overnight

Transfer the dried fruit and soya milk into a food processor and blend into a smooth consistency

Add the flax seed oil and blend again

Divide the mixture between 4 glass dishes and refrigerate until set

Decorate each serving with a sliced strawberry and serve with coconut soya yoghurt

**Blueberry and pear slump**

2 large ripe pears, peeled, cored and chopped
200g or 7 oz blueberries
5 tbsp caster sugar
175g or 6 oz plain flour
1 tsp baking powder
50g or 2 oz ground almonds
25g or 1 oz Vitalite spread, diced
150ml or 5 fl oz almond milk
25g or 1 oz flaked almonds

Divide the blueberries and the pear chunks between 4 large ramekins abnd sprinle with 2 tbsp of the sugar

Sift the flour and the baking powder together into a bowl and stir in the ground almonds and 2 tbsp of the remaining sugar

Add the spread and rub in with your fingertips

Then stir in the almond milk to make a sticky dough

Dot small spoonsfuls of the dough over the fruit and sprinkle over the remaining tbsp of sugar and the flaked almonds

Bake in a preheated oven at 190°C or 375°F or gas mark 5, for 25- 30 minutes until the fruit is soft and the topping is golden

# Banana and strawberry ice cream

525g 1 lb 3 oz carton of soya vanilla custard
250 ml or 8 fl oz soya cream
3 bananas, roughly chopped
175g or 6 oz hulled strawberries
3 tbsp Canadian maple syrup

Blend the custard, cream, bananas, half of the strawberries and the Canadian maple syrup together in a food processor until smooth

Poor the mixture into a freezer proof container and freeze for 3 hours until just starting to freeze around the edges

Scrape the mixture into a bowl and beat with a spatula until smooth

Finely chop the remaining strawberries, stir into the mixture and return to the container

Freeze for another 3- 4 hours or overnight until firm

Allow to soften for 15 minutes before serving

*We worked for a while to give Jacob a proper taste of ice cream not just a sorbet. I make this sometimes as a treat, but he really loves the vegan Magnum ice cream lollies that have came out recently.*

# Grilled vegetables and couscous

Couscous
1 large aubergine
2 large courgettes
2 red peppers, cored, deseeded and quartered
4 tbsp olive oil
200g or 7 oz couscous
450 ml or ¾ pint boiling vegetable stock
50g or 2 oz Vitalite
2 tbsp chopped mixed herbs, such as mint, coriander and parsley
Juice of 1 lemon
Salt and black pepper

For the tahini yoghurt sauce
125g or 4 oz Greek style soya yoghurt
1 tbsp tahini paste
1 garlic clove, crushed
½ tbsp lemon juice
1 tbsp extra virgin olive oil


Cut the aubergine and courgettes into 5mm or ¼ inch thick slices and put in a large bowl with the red peppers

Add the olive oil and salt and pepper and stir well

Heat a ridged griddle pan until hot, then add the vegetables, in batches and cook for 3-4 minutes on each side, depending on size, until charred and tender

Put the couscous in a heatproof bowl, then pour over the boiling vegetable stock, cover and then leave to soak for 5 minutes

Fluff up the grains with a fork and stir in the Vitalite, herbs, lemon juice and salt and pepper to taste

Then combine all the tahini yoghurt sauce ingredients

Season with the salt and pepper

Serve with the vegetables and couscous

You can also crush 2 garlic cloves into 150g or 5 oz of real mayonnaise and serve with the vegetables and couscous

## New potato, basil and pine nut salad

1 kg or 2 lb new potatoes, scrubbed
4 tbsp extra virgin olive oil
1 ½ tbsp white wine vinegar
50g or 2 oz pine nuts, toasted
½ bunch of basil leaves
Salt and pepper

Cook the potatoes for 12- 15 minutes in lightly salted boiling water in a large saucepan

Drain well and transfer to a large bowl

Cut any large potatoes in half

Whisk the oil, vinegar and a little salt and pepper together in a small bowl

Add half of the dressing to the potatoes and allow to cool completely

Then add the pine nuts, the remaining of the dressing and the basil

Stir well and serve

**Traditional potato salad**

1 kg or 2 lb new potatoes, scrubbed
150 or ¼ pint of real mayonnaise
1 bunch of finely chopped spring onions
2 tbsp fresh chives, chopped
A squeeze of lemon juice
Salt and pepper

Cook the potatoes for 12- 15 minutes in lightly salted boiling water in a large saucepan

Drain well and transfer to a large bowl

Cut any large potatoes in half

Mix the mayonnaise, the spring onions, the chopped chives, a squeeze of lemon juice and the salt and pepper

Then toss with the cooked potatoes and serve

# Crusty white loaf

450g 1 lb strong white bread flour, plus extra for dusting
1 ½ tsp fast action dried yeast
300 ml or 10 fl oz tepid water
1 tsp salt
1 tsp sugar
1 tbsp sunflower oil, plus extra for oiling


Stir the flour and yeast together in a large mixing bowl

Then mix in the salt and the sugar

Mix to form a soft dough, adding a little more water if required

Turn out on to a lightly floured work surface and knead the dough for 5- 10 minutes until smooth and elastic

Shape the dough into a round by tucking all of the edges into the middle, then place in a large oiled boil, smooth side up

Cover loosely with oiled cling film and leave in a warm place for 1 hour, or until it has doubled in size

Oil and flour the inside of the loaf tin, tapping pout the excess flour

When the dough has risen, lightly knead the dough and press it into a rectangle shape

Tuck the shorter ends in, followed by the longer edges, then lay it, seem side down in the loaf tin

Cover loosely with the oiled cling film and leave for 30 minutes, or until risen

Preheat the oven to 220°C or 425°F or gas mark 7

Dust the top of the loaf with some flour then slash the top with a sharp knife and then bake for 20 minutes

Then reduce the oven to 200°C or 400°F or gas mark 6 and bake for a further 20 minutes, until well risen with a golden crust

Turn out the loaf and check that it is cooked, it will sound hollow when tapped on the base, transfer to a wire rack to cool

# Rich chocolate biscuit

100g or 3 ½ oz Vitalite softened
50g or 1 ¾ caster sugar
125g or 4 ½ oz plain flour
25g or 1 oz cocoa powder
Melted dairy free chocolate to drizzle

Preheat the oven to 180°C or 250°F or gas mark 4

Line 2 baking trays with baking parchment

In a large mixing bowl cream together the Vitalite and the sugar until pale and creamy

Then sift in the flour and the cocoa powder and beat until the mixture comes together to form a dough

Bring it together with your hands at the end

Roll the dough into 16 walnut sized balls and place it on the baking trays

Press each ball with the prongs of a fork

The bake for 20 minutes

Once baked transfer on to a wire rack to cool completely

Then melt chocolate in a glass mixing bowl over boiling water and drizzle the melted chocolate over the biscuits and allow to set before serving

*The photograph to the left is of the chocolate biscuits. I had no chocolate to melt so we didn't drizzle these cookies in melted chocolate, but they were still super tasty.*

## Strawberry and lavender crush

400g or 13 oz fresh strawberries
2 tbsp icing sugar, plus extra for dusting
4 -5 lavender flower stems, plus extra to decorate
400g 13 oz of Greek style soya yoghurt
4 ready- made meringue nests

Reserve 4 small strawberries for decoration

Hull the rest of the strawberries then put them and the sugar in a food processor and blend to a smooth puree

Pull off the lavender flowers from the stems and crumble them into the puree to taste

Put the soya yoghurt in a bowl and then crumble in the meringues, then lightly mix together

Add the strawberry puree and fold together with a spoon until marbled

Spoon into 4 dessert glasses

Slice the reserved strawberries into a fan, then use with the lavender flowers to decorate the desserts

Then lightly dust with icing sugar and serve immediately

# Butternut squash soup

3 small butternut squash, about 1.7kg or 3 ½ lb total weight
2 tbsp olive oil
Grated nutmeg
Salt and black pepper
30g or 1 oz Vitalite
1 large onion, roughly chopped
2 large carrots, roughly chopped
2 large celery stalks, roughly chopped
1.2- 1.3 litres or 2- 2 ¼ pints of vegetable stock
Crusty bread to serve


Cut each squash lengthways in half, then scoop out and discard the seeds and stringy fibres

Arrange the squash halves cut side up in a roasting tin just large enough told them in a single layer

Drizzle the oil over the flesh of the squash, and season with the nutmeg, salt and pepper

Pour 150ml or ¼ pint of cold water into the tin around the squash

Roast in a preheated oven at 200°C or gas mark 6 for about 1 hour until tender

Then remove from the oven and set aside until cool enough to handle

Meanwhile melt the Vitalite in a large saucepan and add the chopped vegetables

Then cook over a high heat for a few minutes until lightly coloured, stirring constantly

Pour in the stock, season with the salt and pepper, and bring to the boil

Cover and simmer gently for 20 minutes or until the vegetables are tender then remove from the heat

Scoop the flesh from the squash from the skins and blend with the stock and vegetables until smooth

Then return the soup to the pan, then reheat, and taste for seasoning, then serve hot with crusty bread

## Peach and rosewater crush

3 fresh peaches, halved and destoned
2 tbsp clear honey
2 tsp rosewater
Crystallized rose petals
Icing sugar for dusting
400g or 13 oz dairy free soya yoghurt
4 ready- made meringue nests

Put the 2 halved peaches in a food processor with the clear honey

Then add the rosewater and blend into a smooth puree

Put the yoghurt in a bowl and then crumble in the meringues and lightly mix together

Add the peach puree mixture and fold with a spoon until marbled

Place the crystallized rose petals on the top of the dessert to decorate

Lightly dust with icing sugar and serve immediately

## Banana and fig filo tart

6 large sheets of jus- rol filo pastry (as its dairy free)
50g or 2 oz Vitalite, melted
4 bananas, sliced
6 dried figs, sliced
25g or 1 oz caster sugar
Grated rind of ½ lemon
½ tsp ground cinnamon
Greek style soya yoghurt with honey


Cut the pastry sheets in half cross ways, then lay one sheet flat on a baking tray and brush with melted Vitalite

Then top with the second sheet and again brush with the melted Vitalite and continue with the remaining sheets

Then arrange the banana and fig slices over the pastry

Mix the sugar, lemon rind and cinnamon, then sprinkle over the fruit and drizzle over the remaining melted butter

Bake in a preheated oven 200°C or 400°F or gas mark 6, for 15 minutes until the pastry is crisp and the fruit is golden

Then serve hot with the Greek style soya yoghurt with honey

## Spiced apple filo tart

6 large sheets of jus- rol filo pastry (as its dairy free)
50g or 2 oz Vitalite, melted
2 apples, cored and thinly sliced
25g or 1 oz caster sugar
½ tsp ground cinnamon
Greek style soya yoghurt with honey

Cut the pastry sheets in half cross ways, then lay one sheet flat on a baking tray and brush with melted Vitalite

Then top with the second sheet and again brush with the melted Vitalite and continue with the remaining sheets

Then arrange the thinly sliced apple over the filo pastry

Mix the sugar and cinnamon, then sprinkle over the apple slices and drizzle over the remaining melted butter

Bake in a preheated oven 200°C or 400°F or gas mark 6, for 15 minutes until the pastry is crisp and the fruit is golden

Then serve hot with the Greek style soya yoghurt with honey

**Roasted tomato and garlic soup**

1kg or 2 lbs ripe tomatoes
2 tbsp olive oil
1 onion, chopped
3 garlic cloves, coarsely chopped
1 ½ litres or 2 ½ pints vegetable stock
Ready- made vegan pesto to serve

Cut the tomatoes in half and arrange them cut side down in a roasting tin

Bake in a preheated oven at 220°C or gas mark 7 for 15 minutes or until the skins are charred

Remove from the oven and leave until they are cool enough to handle, then peel off the skins and discard the skins

Chop the tomato flesh coarsely, retaining the juice

Then heat the oil in a large saucepan over a medium heat and add in the onion and the garlic, cook gently for a few minutes stirring occasionally, until soft but not coloured

Then add the stock and the tomato flesh and juices, then bring to the boil, lower the heat and simmer for 5 minutes, then add the salt and pepper to taste

Serve the soup hot, with a bowl of pesto so everyone can stir in a spoonful before they eat

# Chicken with sage and orange

4 boneless chicken breasts, with the skin on
1 tbsp plain flour
Orange segments and fresh sage leaves to garnish

Marinade
300ml or ½ pint orange juice
1 tbsp light soy sauce
2 garlic cloves, crushed
2 tbsp chopped fresh sage
1 cm or ½ inch piece if fresh root ginger, peeled and grated
Salt and black pepper

Make the marinade, combine the orange juice, soy sauce, garlic, sage, ginger and salt and pepper

Toss the chicken in the marinade, cover and leave to marinate in the fridge for 20- 30 minutes

Reserve the marinade, and arrange the chicken breasts, skin- side up, in a large roasting tin

Then roast the chicken in a preheated oven at 190°C or gas mark 5 for 10 minutes or until the chicken is cooked through

Remove the chicken with a slotted spoon, and arrange on a warmed platter, then cover and keep warm

Pour all but 2 tbsp of the marinade I not a jug and reserve then add the flour to the remaining marinade in the roasting tin and mix to a smooth paste

Put the roasting tin on the hob, and cook stirring for 1 minute, gradually stirring in the reserved marinade

Bring to a boil, simmer for 2 minutes, and then taste for seasoning

Strain, pour a little around the chicken breasts and garnish with the orange segments and fresh sage

Serve with new potatoes and tender stem broccoli and serve with the remaining sauce separately

**Turkey to go**

500g or 1 lb turkey breast fillets, cut into thin strips
1 tsp ground coriander
1 tsp ground cumin
Salt and black pepper
8 soft tortilla wraps
2 tbsp sunflower oil
1 red bell pepper, halved, seeded and thinly sliced

To serve
Shredded romaine lettuce
Tomato salsa
Soya Greek yoghurt

Put the turkey strips in a bowl with the coriander and cumin

Season with salt and pepper, then mix well to coat the turkey pieces in the spices

Cover and marinade in the fridge for at least 30 minutes, more if time allows

Warm the tortillas, sprinkle the tortillas with water and stack them, then wrap them in foil and warm them in a preheated oven at 140°C or gas mark 1 for 10 minutes

Then heat the oil in a wok and fry the turkey strips with red pepper strips in batches until golden brown and cooked through, for about 4 minutes

You may need to add more oil after each batch

Transfer the warm tortillas to a plate and add the turkey and peppers to a serving dish

Let each person spread their tortillas with the plain yoghurt and salsa and top this with the shredded lettuce and turkey, then roll into a flat cigar shape

Then enjoy

**Mushroom stroganoff**

20g or ¾ dried porcini mushrooms
2 tbsp olive oil
1 onion, chopped
1 garlic clove, crushed
500g 1 lb chestnut mushrooms
2 red peppers, halved, seeded, and sliced
2 tsp paprika
Salt and black pepper
30g or 1 oz cornflour
300ml or ½ pint cold vegetable stock
1 x 400g can of artichoke hearts, drained
2 tbsp dry white wine
1 tbsp tomato puree
Plain soya yoghurt

Soak the dried mushrooms in 150ml or ¼ pint warm water for 20 minutes, then drain and reserve the soaking water

Heat the oil in a flameproof casserole, then add the onion and the garlic and then cook 3-5 minutes until softened

Then add the mushrooms, peppers and paprika and season with the salt and pepper

Then cook, stirring occasionally for 5 minutes

Mix the cornflour and stock, add to the pan with the artichokes, wine, mushroom water, and tomato puree and bring to a boil

Simmer gently for 10- 15 minutes, taste for seasoning and serve hot with the plain yoghurt

## Mixed berry pancakes with coconut

For the pancakes
2oog or 7 oz plain flour
1 tbsp ground flaxseed
2 tsp baking powder
¼ tsp salt
1 tsp granulated sugar
300 ml or 10 fl oz sweetened soya milk
1 tsp vanilla extract
Sunflower oil for cooking

For the topping
4 tbsp raspberry jam
1 handful desiccated coconut
2 tbsp water
2 handfuls blueberries
2 handfuls strawberries, halved

Or lemon juice and sugar

Or real Canadian maple syrup

For the topping, heat the jam, coconut and water in a small pan then set aside

Mix all the pancake batter ingredients together in a glass jug and blend together or whisk to remove bubbles

Add 2 tbsp of sunflower oil in a frying pan and ladle 4 tbsp of batter at a time into the frying pan

Allow the pancake to spread naturally

Cook for 3 minutes, then turn over and cook for a further 3minutes until each side is golden brown

Then serve the pancakes on a serving plate with the topping in a jug, with the choice of the maple syrup or the lemon and sugar

## French toast

250 ml or 8 fl oz sweetened soya milk
6 tbsp plain flour
2 tbsp maple syrup, plus extra drizzling
½ tsp ground cinnamon
1 tsp vanilla extract
8 slices of bread
Sunflower oil, for frying
Big handful of blueberries
Icing sugar

Whisk together the milk, flour and maple syrup in a wide shallow dish

Then add the cinnamon and vanilla and mix together

Then dip both sides of the slice of bread into the batter, cook one slice of French toast at a time

Heat 2 tbsp of sunflower oil in a frying pan, over a medium heat

Cook each slice of French toast for 3 minutes on each side until golden brown

Add a little more oil, if necessary

Serve drizzled with maple syrup and top with blueberries and serve dusted with icing sugar

## Rainbow oven fries

2 large potatoes, peeled
1 large beetroot, peeled
1 large sweet potato, peeled
1 large carrot, peeled
1 large parsnip, peeled
3 tbsp olive oil
Sweet chilli sauce or tomato ketchup to serve

Preheat the oven to 200°C or 400°F or gas mark 6

Cut each vegetable into 1 cm or ½ inch thick slices, then cut each slice into 1 cm or5 ½ inch fries

Then toss the fries with the olive oil and the salt

Arrange the fries in a single layer in 1- 2 baking trays

Bake for 45 minutes, turning them over every 15 minutes until lightly browned and cooked through

Serve with sweet chilli sauce or ketchup

## Potato dauphinoise

3 garlic cloves, peeled
500 ml or 18 fl oz soya cream
500 ml or 18 fl oz unsweetened milk
Large pinch salt
8 large King Edward or Maris Piper potatoes, peeled and very thinly sliced, about 3 mm or ½ inch thick

Preheat the oven to 190°C or 375°C or gas mark 5

Gently squash the garlic with the back of a wooden spoon

Put the cream, milk, garlic and salt into a large pan and bring to a simmer

Add the potatoes and simmer, gently stirring, for 3 minutes until just cooked

Then remove the potatoes with a slotted spoon and place them in a shallow ovenproof dish so that they are about 5cm or 2 inches in depth

Discard the garlic from the sauce and pour over the potatoes, just enough to cover all the slices

Bake for 30 minutes until the potatoes are soft and browned on top

*Such a creamy and delicious side dish, it's great for special occasions and look good served at the table in the oven dish.*

# Mushroom and red wine pâté

3 large slices of white bread, crusts removed
2 tsp sunflower oil
1 small onion, peeled and finely chopped
1 garlic clove, peeled and crushed
350g or 12 oz button mushrooms, wiped and finely chopped
150 ml or ¼ pint of red wine
½ tsp dried mixed herbs
1 tbsp freshly chopped parsley
Salt and freshly ground black pepper
2 tbsp vegan cream cheese

To serve
Finely chopped cucumber
Finely chopped tomato


Preheat the oven to 180°C or 350°C or gas mark 4

Cut the bread diagonally, then place the bread triangles on a baking tray and cook for 10 minutes

Remove from the oven and split each triangle in half to make 12 triangles and return to the oven until golden and crisp

Then leave to cool on a wire rack

Heat a little oil in a saucepan and gently cook the onion and garlic until the onion is soft and transparent

Then add the mushrooms and cook, stirring for 3- 4 minutes

Stir in the wine and the herbs and then bring to the boil

Reduce the heat a little and simmer uncovered until all of the liquid is absorbed

Then remove from the heat and season to taste with salt and pepper then allow to cool

Once cold beat in the began cream cheese and again taste and add extra seasoning if required

Then serve in a small clean, chilled bowl, serve with the toast triangles and the cucumber and tomato

# Vegetables braised in olive oil and lemon

Small strip lemon rind of ½ lemon
Juice of ½ lemon
4 tbsp olive oil
1 bay leaf
Large sprig of thyme
150 ml or ¼ pint of water
4 spring onions trimmed and finely chopped
175g or 6 oz baby button mushrooms
175g or 6 oz broccoli, cut into small florets
175g or 6 oz cauliflower, cut into florets
1 medium courgette, sliced on the diagonal
2 tbsp freshly snipped chives
Salt and freshly ground black pepper
Lemon zest, to garnish


Put the parcd lemon rind and juice into a large saucepan

Add the olive oil, bay leaf, thyme and the water, then bring to the boil

Then add the spring onions and mushrooms

Top with the broccoli and cauliflower, trying to add them so that the stalks are submerged in the water and the tops are just above it

Cover and simmer for 3 minutes

Scatter the courgettes on top, so that they are steamed rather than boiled

Cook, covered for a further 3- 4 minutes, until all the vegetables are tender

Using a slotted spoon, transfer the vegetables from the liquid into a warmed serving dish

Then increase the heat and boil rapidly for 3- 4 minutes, until the liquid is reduced to about 8 tbsp

Remove the lemon rind, bay leaf and thyme sprig and discard

Stir the snipped chives into the reduced liquid, season to taste with salt and pepper and pour over the vegetables

Sprinkle with lemon zest and serve immediately

## Pizza pittas

1 tbsp olive oil
1 garlic clove, peeled and crushed
100g or 3 ½ oz can chopped tomatoes
2 sun dried tomatoes, in oil or rehydrated, chopped
1 tsp dried oregano
Pinch of salt
Pinch of sugar
4 pitta breads
2 large tomatoes, sliced
100g or 3 ½ oz mozzarella style vegan Sheese
Basil leaves


Preheat the oven to 200°C or 400°F or gas mark 6

Heat the olive oil in a pan over a medium heat and cook the garlic for 1 minute

Then add the chopped tomatoes and the sun dries tomatoes

Then add the oregano, salt and sugar, and cook for 10 minutes

Once the tomatoes mixture is cooked, blend into a smooth sauce

Then spread a layer of sauce on to the pitta bread

Add the sliced tomato and vegan mozzarella style vegan Sheese

You could add any other desired topping here such as sliced mushroom, ham, cooked bacon or even pineapple

Cook the pizza pittas for 10- 15 minutes and add the ripped up basil leaves to serve

*The pizza pittas are a great dinner time treat, especially if I purchase the pitta bread, they are also then very quick and easy. Another one of little man's favourites.*

# Rocket and potato soup with garlic croutons

700g or 1 ½ lbs baby new potatoes
1.1 litres or 2 pints vegetable stock
50g or 2 oz rocket leaves
125g or 4 oz thick white sliced bread
50g or 4 oz Vitalite
1 tsp ground nut oil
2- 4 garlic cloves, peeled and chopped
125g or 4 oz stale ciabatta bread, with the crusts removed
4 tbsp olive oil
Salt and freshly ground black pepper
2 tbsp vegan parmesan style Sheese, finely grated

Place the potatoes in a large saucepan, cover with the vegetable stock and simmer gently for 10 minutes

Then add the rocket leaves and simmer for a further 5- 10 minutes until the potatoes are soft and the rocket has wilted

Meanwhile, make the croutons; cut the thick white sliced bread into small cubes and reserve

Heat the Vitalite and ground nut oil in a small frying pan and cook the garlic for 1 minutes, stirring well

Then remove the garlic, then add the bread cubes to the Vitalite and oil mixture in the frying pan and sauté, stirring occasionally, until they are golden brown

Drain the croutons on absorbent kitchen paper and reserve

Cut the ciabatta bread into small dice and stir into the soup

Cover the saucepan and leave to stand for 10 minutes, or until the bread has absorbed a lot of the liquid

Stir in the olive oil, season to taste with salt and pepper and serve at once with a few of the garlic croutons scattered over the top and a little of the grated vegan parmesan style Sheese

# Cream of pumpkin soup

900g or 2 lb pumpkin flesh, after peeling and discarding the seeds
4 tbsp olive oil
1 large onion, peeled
1 leek, trimmed
1 carrot, peeled
2 celery stalks
4 garlic cloves, peeled and crushed
1.7 litres or 3 pints of water
Salt and freshly ground black pepper
¼ tsp freshly grated nutmeg
150 ml or ¼ pint Alpro single cream
¼ tsp cayenne pepper
Warm herby bread, to serve

Cut the skinned and deseeded pumpkin flesh into 2.5 cm or 1 inch cubes

Heat the olive oil in a large saucepan and cook the pumpkin for 2- 3 minute, coating it completely with oil

Chop the onion and leek finely and then cut the carrot and celery into small dice

Add the vegetables to the saucepan with the garlic and cook, stirring, for 5 minutes, or until they have begun to soften

Cover the vegetables with the water and bring to the boil

Season with plenty of salt and pepper and the nutmeg, cover and simmer for 15- 20 minutes until all of the vegetables are tender

When the vegetables are tender, remove from the heat and cool slightly

Then liquidise to form a smooth puree, then pass through a sieve into a clean saucepan

Adjust the seasoning to taste and add all but 2 tbsp of the Alpro cream and enough water to obtain the correct consistency

Bring the soup to boiling point, then add the cayenne pepper and serve immediately swirled with the remaining vegan cream and warm herby bread

## Mushroom and sherry soup

4 slices day- old white bread
Zest ½ lemon
1 tbsp lemon juice
Salt and freshly ground black pepper
125g or 4 oz assorted wild mushrooms, lightly rinsed
125g or 4 oz button mushrooms, wiped
2 tsp olive oil
1 garlic clove, peeled and crushed
6 spring onions, trimmed and diagonally sliced
600 ml or 1 pint vegetable stock
4 tbsp dry sherry
1 tbsp freshly snipped chives, to garnish

Preheat the oven to 180°C or 350°F or gas mark 4

Remove the crusts from the bread and cut the bread into small cubes

In a large bowl toss the cubes on to a lightly oiled, large baking tray and bake for 20 minutes until golden and crisp

If the wild mushrooms are small, leave some whole; otherwise thinly slice all the mushrooms and reserve

Heat the oil in a saucepan, add the garlic and spring onions and cook for 1- 2 minutes

Add the mushrooms and cook  for 3- 4 minutes until they start to soften

Then add the vegetable stock and stir to mix

Bring to the boil, then reduce the heat to gentle simmer, cover and cook for 10 minutes

Stir in the sherry, and season to taste with a little salt and pepper

Pour into warmed bowls, sprinkle over the chives, and serve immediately with the lemon croutons

**Italian bean soup**

2 tsp olive oil
1 leek, washed and chopped
1 garlic clove, peeled crushed
2 tsp dried oregano
75g or 3 oz green beans, trimmed and cut into bitesize pieces
410g can cannellini beans, drained and rinsed
75g or 3 oz small pasta shapes
1 litre or 1 ¾ pint vegetable stock
8 cherry tomatoes
Salt and freshly ground black pepper
3 tbsp freshly shredded basil

Heat the oil in a large saucepan, then add the leek, the garlic and oregano and cook gently for 5 minutes, stirring occasionally

Stir in the green beans and the cannellini beans and then sprinkle in the pasta

Then pour over the vegetable stock

Bring the stock mixture to the boil, then reduce the heat to a simmer

Cook for 12- 15 minutes or until the vegetables are tender and the pasta is cooked to al dente, stirring occasionally

In a heavy based frying pan, dry fry the tomatoes over a high heat until they soften, and the skins begin to blacken

Gently crush the tomatoes in the pan with the back of a spoon and add to the soup

Season to taste with salt and pepper, stir in the shredded basil and serve immediately

## Grandad Terry's Fruit Cake

*Makes a 8-inch cake best used with a 10-inch cake board*
907g or 2lb Mixed fruit
43g or 1 ½ oz mixed peel
43g or 1 ½ oz flaked almonds
85g or 3 oz glace cherries
½ tbsp mixed spice
200g or 7 oz plain flour
200g or 7 oz brown sugar
200g or 7 oz Vitalite dairy free margarine
Juice of 1 lemon
large eggs x3
2    tbsp cocoa powder


Preheat the oven to 200°C or gas mark 6
Cream together the margarine and the sugar until light and fluffy
Sieve the flour and the cocoa butter and the mixed spice
Beat the eggs
Then gradually beat in the flour and the eggs alternatively until all mixed together
Stir in the mixed peel
Stir in the mixed fruit
Stir in the almonds, cherries and lemon juice
Grease and line an 8 inch cake tin with Vitalite and greaseproof paper
Poor in the mixture then level it off and make a well in the centre
Turn the oven down to 180°C or gas mark 3 and cook for 1 hour
Then cook for 2nd hour at 150°C or gas mark 2
Then cook for a 3rd hour at 140°C or gas mark 1
Then cook for a fourth and final hour at 130°C or gas mark ½
Check by inserting a skewer into the centre of the cake, if it come out clean then it is done
Let the cake cool in the tin and turn out ready to decorate as desired

*The images are from our wedding day of the wedding cake my Father-in-law made for us.*

It is handmade and beautifully hand decorated by Jacob's Grandad Terry.

It was delicious, he also added brandy in with the mixed fruit for our cake and it was gorgeous.

I also still have the beautiful diamante heart from on the top.

Printed in Great Britain
by Amazon